Knit a Hat

Knit a Hat

A Beginner's Guide to Knitting

Alanna Okun

ABRAMS, NEW YORK

Editor: Meredith A. Clark

Series Designer: Laura Palese

Designer:
Shawn Dahl, dahlimama inc

Production Manager:
Kathleen Gaffney

Library of Congress
Control Number: 2020931037

ISBN: 978-1-4197-4065-7
eISBN: 978-1-64700-113-1

Abrams books are available at
special discounts when purchased
in quantity for premiums and
promotions as well as fundraising
or educational use. Special
editions can also be created to
specification. For details, contact
specialsales@abramsbooks.com or
the address below.

Abrams® is a registered trademark
of Harry N. Abrams, Inc.

ABRAMS The Art of Books
195 Broadway, New York, NY 10007
abramsbooks.com

3 Making the Hat 75

Welcome to Knitting!

Why Knitting?

There are so many reasons to learn to knit. Maybe you've been in search of a hobby, an activity to keep your hands busy with something other than scrolling mindlessly through your phone or picking at your nails on your daily commute. Something more outwardly focused than meditation but more inward than watching movies; lower impact than exercise; cheaper and healthier than a vat of red wine.

Maybe you find yourself needing a process that's tangible, one that involves taking little more than sticks and string, adding time and effort, and ending with a real, useful object.

Maybe the older you get, the more you realize it's been a really long time since you've learned something new, and figure you should give being a beginner a try again, with exceptionally low stakes. Maybe you feel like it's time to just suck at something for a little while.

Or maybe you just really want a hat!

Whatever your reasoning—and there are infinitely more options than I've mentioned—wanting to learn to knit means you're already well on your way there. You might think you're not "crafty" or capable of wrapping your brain around it, but I can assure you that in my ten-odd years of teaching knitting to other people, I've had more students than I can count who make the exact same claim and walk away from their first (sometimes second) lesson with an honest-to-God piece of fabric. It might be a little crooked, it might not yet be a scarf or a hat, it might not look like something you'd see on Instagram or pick up in a clothing store, but it's the essential building block for everything that's to come. I promise that whether you're left- or right-handed, an experienced maker of things or a total klutz, you are more than capable of getting there too.

Why a Hat?

Eventually, of course, you'll want that scrap of fabric, or one like it, to actually become a thing. The most popular such item, in knitting lessons and lore, is a scarf.

This makes a lot of sense on the surface. A scarf is the easiest beginner project to knit inasmuch as to make the most basic scarf, all you need to learn is to cast on (we'll get to that), to do the knit stitch (that too), and to cast off (I would never leave you hanging).

A scarf is essentially a long practice swatch, and therein lies the problem—a scarf can be very, very long. For some beginners, this is a good thing; performing the same motion over and over again gets them in the correct rhythm, helps them improve and troubleshoot their own work as they go, and generally feels soothing.

For many others, though, repetition is the kiss of death. They start off with great enthusiasm, but by the time they've reached inch ten or so, they begin to wonder precisely how much longer they'll have to do the exact same thing. They'll zone out and drop a stitch or two, which is not a stumbling block on its own but, when it's the result of boredom, is a symptom of a far worse condition. They'll put the project aside for a couple of days that turn into a couple of months that turn into "oh yeah, I tried to knit once, but it just wasn't for me."

This is why, whenever possible, I direct new knitters to try a hat for their first project. This isn't to say that you have to dive in headfirst (ha!)—we'll go over the motions of knit- ting before setting our sights on the full undertaking—but it *is* to say that you'll be a little more challenged than your scarf-knitting counterparts. Making something round, some- thing that requires decreases, is necessarily a tad harder than just going back and forth, but it's the kind of difficulty that you'll learn from. Once you've made a hat, you'll be well set up to make projects you've likely never dared to think about—infinity scarves, sweaters, even socks. Those essen- tial building blocks of knitting that add up to an intricate, lacy top aren't really any different from the ones that will make up your simple, solid hat.

It Will Be Wonky

Still, I understand the fear that creeps in with starting anything new, particularly as an adult. We're taught that we're supposed to be automatically good at whatever we try, and that if we're not, we should abandon it and spend our time doing something else.

But I'd like to argue in favor of being bad at an activity, at least at the beginning; it's not an indictment of you or your worth, and it doesn't mean that you're not "crafty" or will never be able to master a given technique. In fact, it can be good to surrender to the process, to *not* feel like you have to be totally in control at any given moment. And if your first couple of rows, or even your first couple of projects, turn out a little wonky, it's not the end of the world. You can always undo the stitches (we'll go over how to do that) and reuse the

yarn, or keep the item as a testament to where you started and, later on, how far you've come.

Ultimately, though, you'll never have a hat until you commit to starting and to sticking with it. And the chances are good that you or someone in your orbit could use one.

HOW TO USE THIS BOOK

This book is intended for absolute beginners, people who may never have even held a pair of knitting needles in their lives. Or maybe you've awkwardly manipulated needles and muddled through the basic knit stitch, but that's where your experience ends. That's why I describe in detail the choices I suggest making and the processes I suggest following, and, ideally, your first step will be to read (or carefully skim) the whole book to get a sense of the scope. (Spoiler alert: It's a much smaller scope than you're probably expecting.) This advice is similar to a chef's suggestion that you read the entire recipe and prep all the ingredients before beginning to cook, except in this case you're also learning how to chop onions, rinse lettuce, and turn on an oven for the first time.

That said, feel free to hop around. If you already have materials at your disposal, and have checked and made sure they're at least in the ballpark of what this pattern calls for, skip ahead to the instructions for how to begin knitting. If you already know how to do the basic knit stitch and are here so that you can try knitting your first project in the round, amazing! Check out the section devoted to the hat pattern. If you

learned to knit a decade ago and are just trying to refresh some creaky memories, read whatever paragraphs jump out as useful to you. This book is meant to be a resource, not a homework assignment, and there's no single right way to utilize it.

Finally, while I wish I could confidently say that everyone who picks up this book will walk away with full knowledge of how to knit, forever, everyone learns differently. Some folks need more visuals than I'm providing here, while others need a flesh-and-blood human to guide their hands and correct them when they're wrong. If you are one of these many people, that doesn't mean you're bad at knitting, or somehow less than people who can read instructions once and replicate them perfectly. Personally, I've never met a recipe I couldn't figure out how to bizarrely set on fire the first time I attempted it.

What it does mean is that you might need some support—whether it's in the form of YouTube videos or a patient friend, neighbor, or local yarn store employee—or just a lot of practice. (If this is you, check out the list of resources I provide at the end.) Knitting is hard! But it's worth it, and the fact that you're here at all shows that you're at least somewhat interested in learning what it can bring to your life. So let's begin!

CHOOSING YOUR MATERIALS

If it's not the motions of knitting that you find daunting, it might be the sheer array of *stuff* that's seemingly required to get started. And all the possible sources for that stuff: There are big-box stores and small independent yarn shops and the donation pile at your local community center—and the random plastic bins of pastel yarn a well-meaning relative foisted on you during a spring cleanout.

Later on in your knitting career, all these options will likely delight rather than terrify you (although your wallet might remain perpetually distressed). Now, though, it's important to narrow down what you want, and not to get distracted by doodads and baubles and yarn with a whole bunch of sparkly stuff woven into it. We'll go step by step through the basic types of needles and yarn that are out there, and which ones you should zero in on for this first project.

If you'd prefer to skip what all the jargon means for now and revisit it later, that's totally fine. Here's the list of what to look for in order to complete the hat in this book. You can order it all online or tell a salesperson at whatever store you visit who'll be happy to help you.

What You'll Need to Make Your Hat

One size US 7 (4.5 mm) circular needle, 16" **(40 cm) long** (I suggest aluminum or another metal, but whatever material you can find is fine)

One set of size US 7 (4.5 mm) double-pointed **needles** (I suggest bamboo, but, as with the circular needle, whatever material you can find is fine)

Two balls, or at least 300 yards (274 m) total, **of medium-thin weight yarn** (aka sport/DK or light worsted—see page 36 for more info), either both in the same color or one each in two colors you like, for contrast (common brands of yarn that work well here include Brooklyn Tweed Arbor, Cascade 220 Superwash, Loops & Threads Impeccable, and Lily Sugar'n Cream)

One yarn needle

If you're interested in what all of this actually means, here's some info on the tools and materials you'll need for this project and beyond.

Needles

There are three primary types of knitting needles: **straight**, **circular**, and **double-pointed**. They come in all kinds of materials, like bamboo and aluminum, and over time you'll figure out which type and feel you like best in which circumstances. You might also find that you prefer a certain type based on your grip, and whether you're dealing with a condition like arthritis or carpal tunnel syndrome.

But, again, no worries about picking favorites now. We're getting through this first foray together.

STRAIGHT NEEDLES

Straight needles are likely what you're familiar with from stock photos and cartoons. They're *the* essential knitting gear, often depicted as made of wood with a ball on one end. They're best for back-and-forth knitting, known as **knitting flat**, which isn't actually just for flat objects like scarves. Many more complicated, tubular items, like sweaters, can be knit flat, in pieces, and sewn up in a process called **seaming**. Still, straight needles are not ideal for a round item with a smaller circumference—like, say, a hat.

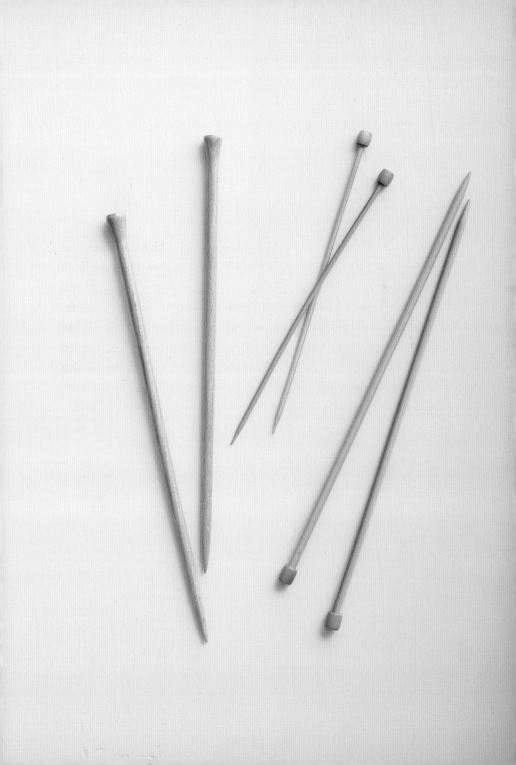

CIRCULAR NEEDLES

Circular needles, on the other hand, are extremely versatile (and my own favorite type) because they can be used to knit flat as well as in a circle, called **knitting in the round**. I barely use straight needles anymore because I prefer, even in flat knitting, to use my circulars; it's basically the same as knitting with two straight needles, but the needles are connected by a length of flexible plastic (called the **cable** or **cord**), which means I can never accidentally lose one. You'll be using a circular needle to knit the hat in this book.

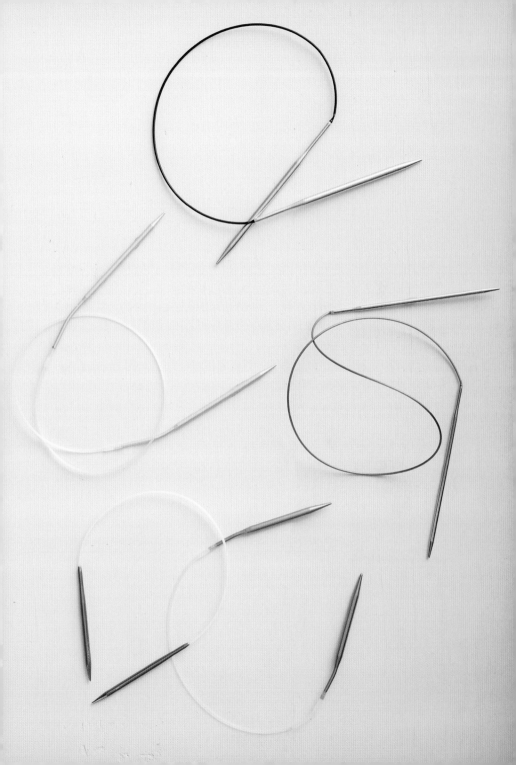

DOUBLE-POINTED NEEDLES

You'll also be using what some knitters regard as the trickiest type of needles: double-pointed needles, or **DPNs**. DPNs are generally used in sets of four or five at a time, and, as the name implies, they have a point on each end. This is so circular items with the smallest circumference, like socks—too small for even the shortest circular needles— can be knit comfortably. Even though it must seem daunting to a new knitter (or an experienced one!) to have to wield five needles at once, it's actually no more difficult than "regular" knitting once you get in the groove. The reason you need them here is that you're going to be knitting the body of the hat on a circular needle and then decreasing the number of stitches in each row as you get closer to the crown, and you'll need to switch over to DPNs in order to get those last few rows done. That's at the very end of the process, though, and by that point you'll have enough facility with knitting that it won't feel nearly as scary as it might right now.

All needles, regardless of type, are sold in **standard sizes**. In the United States, these sizes are numbered, from 000 (extra super tiny, like toothpicks) all the way up to 50 (essentially broom handles). These numbered sizes have corresponding metric sizes, which indicate the needles' diameters, and which you'll find on the packaging and usually on the needles themselves: A size US 4 needle is the same as a 3.5 mm needle, a size US 5 equals a 3.75 mm needle, and so on. (Whether the number is in US sizing will always be specified, because different countries have different numbering systems. The system in use in the United Kingdom, for example, runs in the opposite direction, so that 000 is the thickest rather than the thinnest needle.)

Which needle size is best for your project depends on the yarn you're working with (and vice versa). Very thin yarn, as you can imagine, tends to be knitted with very thin needles. If you were to use a medium or a thick needle, you would create something that looks more like a loose net than a structured piece of fabric. Plenty of knitters use this to their advantage, "mismatching" needles and yarn in order to play around with texture, but for now we're going to play it pretty straight. (There's more on how to find out which needles your yarn calls for in the following section.)

Circular needles also come in varying **lengths**. Standard lengths include 16" (40 cm), which you'll be using here, and 24" (60 cm) and 32" (80 cm), both of which are useful for larger projects like sweaters or cowls. So when I say to find a size US 7 16" circular needle, that means you want the tips to be size 7 and the length (measured from tip to tip) to be 16". It's not at all unreasonable to think when you see size US 7 16" that you should look for a size US 16 needle, except that, for whatever arcane reason, that size doesn't exist. The US numbering goes straight from 15 to 17.

This should, I hope, make your shopping easier. Remember to buy both DPNs and a circular needle. Once you have those, you'll be set up for tons of knitting projects to come.

Yarn

I could easily fill this book talking about different types of yarn: their origins, their feel, what projects they're good for, and with what projects they should under no circumstances be mentioned in the same breath. But for your purposes as a beginner, the most important thing is to figure out what, exactly, you're looking at and how to interpret it.

The best information won't necessarily come from the yarn itself—although, of course, that's important—but, rather, from its label. Whether the yarn comes in a **ball**, a long, twisty **skein**, or a tightly coiled **cake**, the label should have some sort of indication of the yarn's thickness, which will determine which needles it should be used with. Note that if it comes in a skein—that is to say, long, unwound lengths of yarn—you should ask the store to wind it for you, which most indie stores will do, free of charge. No need to wrestle with yarn before you've even started knitting!

CAKE

BALL

SKEIN

Not all labels are alike. Some contain a lot of info and will tell you specifically whether a yarn is considered to be thin by using words like **lace weight**, **sock weight**, or **fingering weight**. Medium-thin yarn will be labeled as **sport weight** or **DK weight**—the one you want for this hat. Medium yarn is typically labeled as **worsted**—another type that'll work here—or **aran**. And thick yarn gets labeled as **chunky**, **bulky**, or **super bulky**. These terms are great for pointing you in the right direction, but don't panic if it's not written right there on the label.

A few craft chains, including Michaels, have also come up with their own, simplified system, demarcating yarn on a scale from 1 (very thin) to 6 (extremely thick). For your hat, look for a 3 on that scale, but a 4 could work as well.

What *will* definitely be readily available on the label is the suggested needle size. It'll likely be given in both US and metric measurements, and there's generally a range of sizes, not just one. So, for example, a DK weight yarn will often call for size US 5–7, or 3.75–4.5 mm, needles.

This range is meant to tell you roughly what your **gauge** for your knitting will be, meaning how many stitches per inch (2.5 cm) you should expect to knit on a given size needle. This matters a lot when it comes to more advanced projects, like form-fitting sweaters and garments with lots of interlocking parts, but less at the outset of your knitting journey. Of course, you don't want your hat to be half (or twice) the circumference of your head, but knitting is stretchy and generally fairly forgiving, so gauge doesn't matter much for the project in this book. Also, everyone's gauge varies, particularly as a beginner, but we'll get to that later.

Right now, all you need to focus on is choosing the yarn. You've got some wiggle room here. As long as the yarn label includes a size US 7 (4.5 mm) needle in its suggested range, you should be fine. Just know that a thicker yarn (say, one calling for size US 7–9 [4.5–5.5 mm] needles) could require a little more wrestling than a thinner one (say, one calling for size US 5–7 [3.75–4.5 mm] or US 6–8 [4–5 mm]) and could produce a somewhat stiffer result.

You'll want at least 300 yards (274 m) of whatever yarn you select. **Yardage**, or exactly how much yarn you're buying, will be included on the label as well (the label will sometimes specify both yards and meters). You might need to buy two of whatever yarn you choose for your hat. You will likely have yarn left over when you're finished, but think of the added yards as an insurance policy against mistakes (which are totally reasonable and to be expected). If you're making a hat for a baby, you'll need far less—closer to 150 yards (137 m)—but it doesn't hurt to have a little extra in case the first hat doesn't turn out the way you want, or if you want to make another.

CHUNKY, OR BULKY, WEIGHT

CHUNKY, OR
BULKY, WEIGHT

DK WEIGHT

FINGERING WEIGHT

SPORT WEIGHT

LACE WEIGHT

WORSTED WEIGHT

Just as important as the technical aspects of yarn are the aesthetics. What yarn is made of matters, both in terms of how it feels to knit and in terms of how it feels to wear. (Not to mention whether it's machine-washable.) A lot of the yarn you'll find at big-box stores like Michaels or JOANN is at least partially made of nonnatural fibers, like **acrylic**. This tends to be less expensive than its natural counterparts and can feel a little more plasticky, or "slippery," as I've heard some knitters call it. Natural-fiber yarns can be found among the offerings at the chain stores and in abundance at independent yarn stores. Try rubbing a strand between your fingers; if the yarn feels too gritty or squeaky, you likely won't enjoy working with it over the course of your project.

Still, I often recommend that my students use acrylic blends with a high content of a natural fiber like **wool**. It's sturdy and often machine-washable (always check the label or ask a sales associate), and it can help mitigate complaints from anyone who thinks wool is too itchy.

Merino wool is generally softer than regular wool, and there's a type called **superwash merino** that can be, you guessed it, put in a washing machine. It's often more expensive but it's a favorite of mine.

There are so many other types of yarn—easy ones to work with like **cotton** and **alpaca**, slightly fussier types like **silk** and **mohair**, expensive strains of **cashmere** and something called **qiviut**, which comes from a musk ox and is an excellent Scrabble word. If you're buying in person, take some time to acquaint yourself with the different types. I, a weirdo, like to rub yarn against my neck to see if it's soft enough for my supersensitive skin, but your own tests may vary.

What I strongly advise against is choosing anything too fluffy or fussy, i.e., something containing a lot of beads or feathers or anything that just looks wildly different from the rest of the yarn on the shelf. Extremely soft, pillowy yarns might be enticing, but they can be tough to wrangle on a first go-round, and they can pill quickly if they're handled too much. Better to stick to more of a workhorse yarn, something soft yet sturdy, and, of course, in a color or two that you absolutely love. Make sure that the color isn't so dark that you won't be able to catch your mistakes. It's more effective to learn from your errors than run from them, tempting as that might be.

Yarn Needle

A yarn needle, also known as a tapestry needle, looks like a giant sewing needle, with an eye wide enough to thread yarn through. Yarn needles typically come in plastic and metal, and don't stress too much over which one to get—whatever they have at the store is likely fine. Also, if it's possible to get more than one for a reduced cost, do it, because they have a habit of vanishing the instant you need them most (which won't be until the very end of your project).

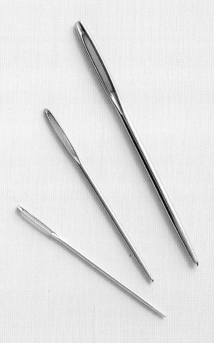

A Note on Cost and Access

Knitting can be an expensive hobby. Even for a project like this one, which requires relatively little investment when compared to the ten or twelve skeins of yarn you might buy to make a sweater, it's not unheard of that the materials alone could cost upward of fifty dollars. That's certainly not nothing, especially considering everyone's financial situation is different, and it can absolutely be a barrier to entry when it comes to learning a new hobby.

To bring the cost down, closer to twenty dollars or about what you'd likely pay for a hat like the one we're going to knit, I recommend these less expensive brands: Susan Bates for both knitting needles and yarn needles (available in most big-box and independent craft stores), Loops & Threads for both yarn and needles (ditto), and Knit Picks for affordable yarn (online at KnitPicks.com). Also, if you have access to a community like a religious group or an education center, or even at your workplace, ask around. I've found that lots of unexpected people have spare craft supplies they'll be happy to give you, and they might even have some stories to share about knitting (or trying to) themselves.

Having to navigate a yarn store where you don't feel welcome can be another barrier to becoming a knitter. I'm a young, thin, cisgendered, nondisabled white woman, and I've never had a negative experience in a crafting environment other than a couple of withering glances from proprietors who likely thought I was a hipster dilettante trying out a twee new hobby for the weekend. That's certainly not the experience of many knitters of color, some of whom have spoken out bravely and passionately in the past few years about feeling excluded from traditionally whitewashed spaces. Nor is it the experience of knitters who can't find patterns sized for their bodies or modified for their particular abilities, or who don't conform to traditional gender norms. Knitting is a part of the world, not separate from it, and the biases, prejudices, and obstacles of that world can still spill over even into this seemingly cozy space.

That's another reason I don't want you to worry too much about getting the "right" supplies—following the guidelines above will likely make your project go more smoothly, but I want knitting to be accessible to everyone, not just people with lots of time and cash to burn and a nearby yarn store they can freely pop into. Hats are forgiving objects, and knitting, while a precise and at times maddening craft, is above all the manipulation of string with sticks, and that activity should be available to everyone who wants to be a part of the community.

LEARNING
THE BASICS

Once you've gathered your materials, block out a couple of (ideally, quiet) hours, if possible. Knitting has a steep learning curve—there's no getting around it—and the odds of quitting out of frustration are a lot higher if you try to do it in dribs and drabs.

Before launching into the hat itself, you're going to knit a **swatch**. A swatch is a piece of fabric you knit to determine what your gauge is—how many stitches you'll make per inch (2.5cm)—and, strictly speaking, it isn't necessary when it comes to making something like a hat where fit doesn't need to be precise. But it comes in handy for our purposes in this book because it is, at the end of the day, a small knitted rectangle, and that's the ideal way to practice for a while before moving on to the main event.

Casting On

Before you can even start knitting that swatch, you have to learn how to get the stitches you'll be knitting onto the needles. This is called **casting on**, and, since this first official step is kind of hard to wrap your head around, it can often be an immediate drop-off point for new knitters. Don't let that happen to you! I promise that once your muscles accept (even just partially) the motions of casting on, you'll be well on your way to actually knitting.

The simplest method of casting on is called the **backwards loop**. If you've ever made a friendship bracelet at camp, you'll have an idea of the theory—it's just a series of little interlocking knots. This is the fastest way to get started, in my teaching experience, but be warned that, when you're not totally used to doing it, it can result in a somewhat loose and sloppy edge. Don't worry too much about that, and also don't feel like you're messing up if it's not perfectly even.

You can use either two of your double-pointed needles or your circular for the swatch. It'll be knit back and forth, not in the round, so go with what feels best right now. I will say that a point in favor of the circular is that it's what you'll use to knit the bulk of the hat (and likely many other projects), but the plastic cable can be a nuisance when you're first learning to cast on, so feel free to use the DPNs if they feel more manageable for now.

If you choose the circular needle, lay it out in front of you, with the plastic cable pointing downward. If you're a righty, use that hand to hold the right-hand tip out in front of you, and vice versa if you're a lefty. The same if you're using the DPNs, except they'll be interchangeable, so no need to worry about which "side" is which; just know that you'll be using your dominant hand to hold the needle that will be receiving the cast-on stitches, and your nondominant hand to make them.

Tie a **slipknot** in the yarn, leaving a tail of about 6 inches (15 cm), and slip it onto the needle, about 1 or 2 inches (2.5 or 5 cm) from the tip. (If the concept of a slipknot is too much to deal with right now, just tie a knot around the needle and nobody will be the wiser.)

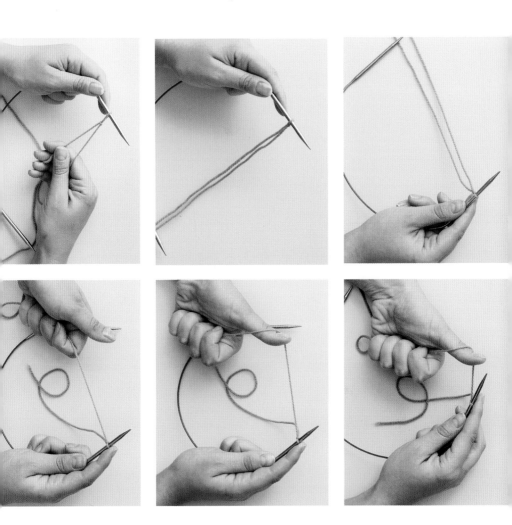

Take the yarn in your nondominant hand—*not* the little tail you've left hanging but the strand that's still attached to the ball of yarn, which is known as the **working yarn**. Referring to the photos (they'll be way more helpful than written instructions), use your thumb to make a loop, flip it around, and slip it onto the tip of the needle.

51

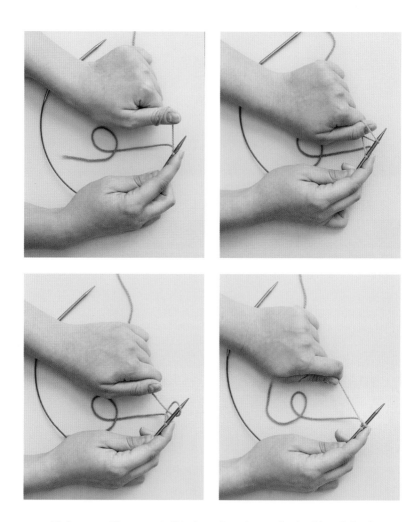

Make sure the yarn tail is hanging down the inside of the loops rather than the outside. Repeat this motion until you have twenty loops on the needles. There is a strong chance this all sounds like nonsense, written out like that. "Loops?!" you might be screaming, internally or externally. "Backward!!!???"

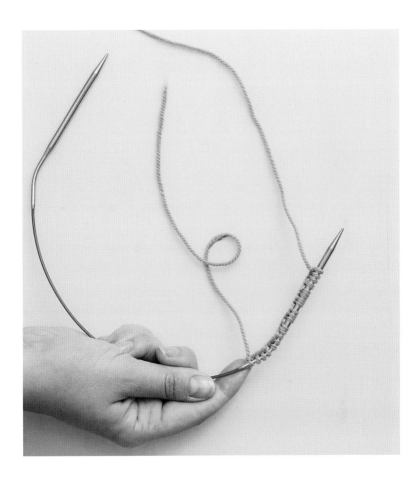

I know, and I genuinely wish I were sitting right there to guide you through this part, because, as I've said, I don't want you to give up just now, or ever. I hope these explanations will be of use, and if mastering the thumb-flick gesture is asking too much, you can use your nondominant hand to pick up the yarn and place it on the needle in the same formation. Basically, as long as you wind up with twenty more or less evenly spaced loops, you're off to a marvelous start.

The Knit Stitch

Again, we're just working on the practice swatch right now, but casting on plus the knit stitch are essentially the only two skills you'll need in order to make your hat (plus a couple of small modifications).

Once you've got those twenty stitches (including your initial slip-knot), turn your work around; that means swap which hands the needles are in, so you've always got the needle with the "old" stitches in your nondominant hand and the one with the "new" stitches (the ones we're about to make) in your dominant. We'll call the needle in your dominant hand the **working needle** from here on out, since it will be where most of the motion happens when it comes to forming those new stitches, and also because "dominant" and "nondominant" are starting not to look like real words anymore.

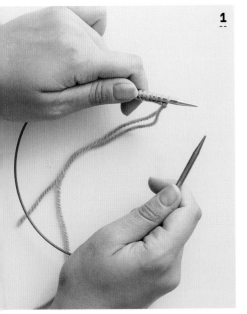 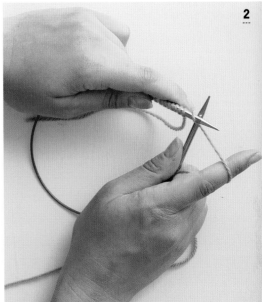

Right now, here's how things should look:

1. Your dominant hand is holding a needle with no stitches on it, while your nondominant hand (see?) is holding the needle with all of them. The first stitch should have the working yarn attached to it, and make sure that yarn is hanging in back rather than in front of the knitting.

2. Push the tip of the working needle through the middle of the first stitch, from front to back. That means the working needle should be underneath the other needle and the yarn should still be at the back of the work.

Hold the yarn with whichever hand feels most comfortable (the answer, right now, will likely be *neither*). There are a couple of schools of thought about which hand you should hold your working yarn with, and how much movement should be involved. As a right-handed person, I tend to hold the yarn in my right hand—the one holding the working needle—and **throw** it over the working needle to form stitches. It's really more like wrapping the yarn around than throwing it, though. This is called the **English method**.

Another widely accepted technique is called **Continental**. When I use this one, I take the yarn in my left hand and hold it tautly over my index finger, making a sort of spool, so that there's always yarn right there for me to knit from. The working needle is used to **pick** the yarn and form stitches, and the majority of the movement happens in that hand while the other remains relatively still.

Continental is regarded as the more speedy and efficient method, but, since I was taught the other way, I've never been able to get as comfortable with Continental as with English knitting. And many of my students have found that it has just one too many new steps to keep in mind. So don't worry about throwing the yarn or picking it, so long as you're getting it where it needs to go. And if you have any hand issues, it could be useful to talk to your doctor or physical therapist about which motion is better for you, since you'll be repeating it many times.

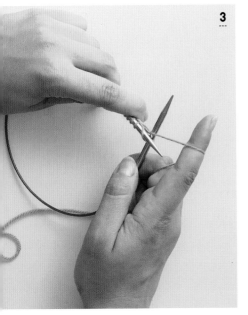 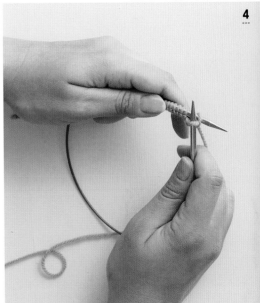

3. From here, holding the yarn however feels best, guide it over the tip of the working needle so it comes up and lies between the two needles, tugging gently so it's not too tight and not too loose. This is the bit of yarn that will form the new stitch, which you're trapping and anchoring with the old one.

4. Carefully draw the tip of the working needle back toward you. This part is a bit fiddly because you don't want to lose the new stitch, but you will need to bring that tip all the way through the old stitch so the tip's now in front instead of in back.

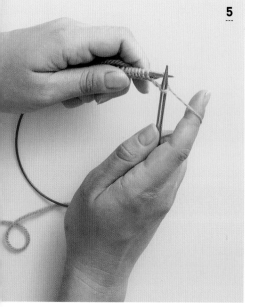 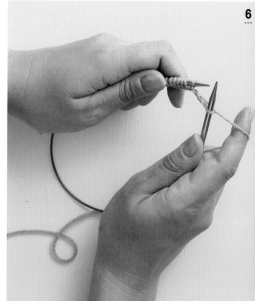

5. Use the working needle to slide the old stitch all the way up to the very tip of the other needle;

6. then let it fall off *that* needle, taking care not to drop any of the other stitches. You've essentially let the stitch "jump" from one needle to the other, only this time it's another row higher. Your needles aren't so much pulling or pushing the yarn as they are sliding in and out of the loops of stitches; you should be moving the needles and the working yarn around much more than you are moving the stitches themselves, which are just sliding from one needle to the other.

That's it! That's your first knit stitch. See if you can finish out the row. Bring the yarn under, over, and through, under-over-through, again and again until it doesn't feel like it takes a full minute to complete one stitch. Be sure to keep your needle tips close together as you continue making your stitches. If you pull them too far apart, you'll get a length of yarn that will turn into an unsightly loop that you'll have to hide later on.

Continue knitting your swatch. Each time you reach the end of a row of stitches, turn the work around and start again, taking care to keep the yarn in back. This is a very important step, because if you don't turn the work around, you'll start knitting in the round.

What you're knitting right now is called **garter stitch**, which means you're knitting every single row. It results in a thick, sturdy fabric with ridges, and it is often used to anchor the edges of knitting projects because it doesn't curl up on itself.

I suggest knitting twenty rows to really get used to it. This should result in ten bumpy little ridges in the piece of fabric. (You can also ignore those numbers and just knit until you get the hang of it, but I like rules and thought you might too.)

The Purl Stitch

Fair warning: If you are an absolute beginner, trying to learn to purl right now could mess you up, and the basic hat pattern you're about to knit purposely doesn't require any purling. But the purl stitch is an invaluable building block and something you'll likely want and need to learn if you stick with knitting, so if you're feeling confident, by all means try it. There's a modification of the pattern that calls for a ribbed brim, which is a little stretchier and sportier-looking than the standard one, and it will be a mix of knit and purl stitches.

The reason purling can derail new knitters is that the purl stitch is the inverse of the knit stitch. This means, for your purposes, that you complete it in essentially the opposite way of what you've been doing up to this point.

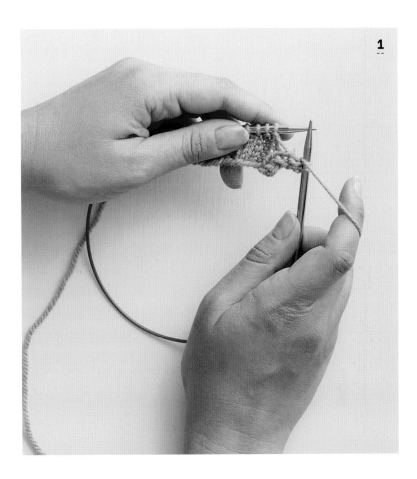

Still, it's ultimately all knitting. Hold your needles in the same way you did in the knit stitch, with the working needle in your dominant hand.

1. This time, though, bring the yarn in front of the work rather than keeping it in back.

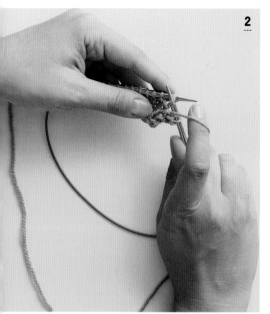

2. Insert the tip of your working needle into the stitch from back to front, top to bottom, instead of from front to back, bottom to top.

3. Wrap the yarn over the tip of the working needle, and use the same motion as in the knit stitch in order to create a new stitch. Carefully draw the tip back toward yourself,

4. "catching" the new stitch

5. and then lifting off the old stitch. It's really not so different after all.

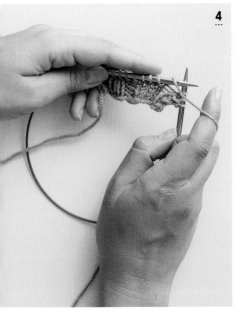

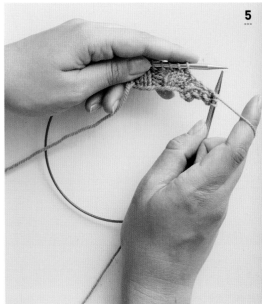

I strongly recommend purling a couple of rows on their own, then knitting a couple of rows, before you attempt them both in the same row; it's all too easy to "unlearn" one as you focus on nailing the other. Eventually, though, you should try doing two knit stitches followed by two purl stitches and repeating that across a row. This is what will constitute **ribbing**, and it will come into play if you want to try that particular hat mod later on.

Trouble-shooting

Again, I wish I were sitting right beside you for all this, since there are many ways for knitting to go wonky that can be diagnosed only by sight. But here are fixes for a few common missteps.

First, what do you do if you **drop a stitch**? It's likely a term you've heard before, and it can seem catastrophic when you're first starting out. It can also *be* catastrophic if left unchecked, because a dropped stitch has the potential to unravel all the way back to the first row of your knitting, leaving an unsightly ladder in the middle of the work. But we are not going to let that happen, and, in addition, nothing that happens in knitting can actually ever be literally catastrophic, because it is just knitting.

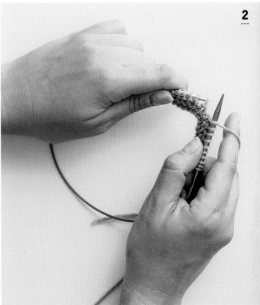

1. If you notice a dropped stitch right when it happens (when, that is, it has either slid off the needle of its own accord or not made the jump from one needle to the other, and is just kind of hanging out there nakedly with nothing to support it),

2. simply pick it back up, with your fingers or with the tip of your needle, and put it back where it belongs. If you'd already managed to complete the stitch, put it on your working needle, and if it fell before you could work the yarn through it, put it back on the other needle and just knit it as usual.

If the dropped stitch is in the middle of the row and/or seems to have dropped down a couple of rungs, wait until you've knitted your way back to where it's fallen and pick it up with the working needle. Then work the tip of that needle underneath the first rung and use the other needle to pass the dropped stitch over that rung, repeating until you're all the way back up at the top. The repair will be a little obvious (for reasons we'll get into later), but the fabric will be intact.

Second, your **stitch count** may be off. If you find that you have way too many or way too few stitches, ensure that what you're knitting is actually supposed to be a stitch. The place where many stitches tend to get duplicated is at the beginning of a new row, because the little "scarf" of yarn that wraps each stitch is especially big and floppy around the first stitch. It's easy to mistake this for a stitch of its own and knit it as such, so take care to knit only directly from the needle. As for vanishing stitches, you could be dropping them or else knitting a couple of stitches together, which is actually a technique you'll be learning to do on purpose when you make the hat. For now, if it feels like you're forcing your needle through too many loops of yarn, you likely are.

And, finally, one of the biggest hurdles new knitters face is determining the proper **tension**, or how tightly to hold the yarn. If you tug too much while making your stitches, it'll be much harder to insert the tip of your needle on the following row; if you leave the yarn too loose, the stitches can look sloppy and uneven. For better or worse, there's not a ton you can do about this at the outset—it's really a problem that solves itself with time and experience.

Just try to stay as aware as you can about how you're holding the yarn. It can feel like the last thing you want to keep in mind when you're already busy remembering in which direction to feed the yarn and how not to accidentally drop all your stitches, but it'll result in more even work, and will with luck give you something calming (or at least less stressful) to fixate on as you get the hang of knitting.

Casting Off

If you were to decide to just stop and yank the needle out from your stitches right now, after your twenty rows, the stitches would probably last no more than five minutes before unraveling. That's why you need to secure them with one of the many methods of **casting off**.

This particular technique is not actually going to be part of making the hat—we'll use a different (and, frankly, even easier) trick to get your final stitches off the needles—but it's a crucial one for any knitter to know, and not at all dissimilar from the knit stitch.

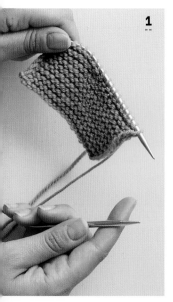

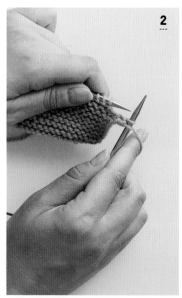

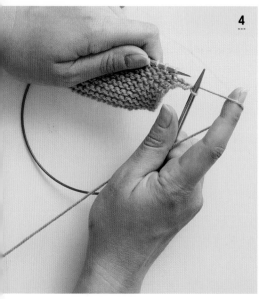

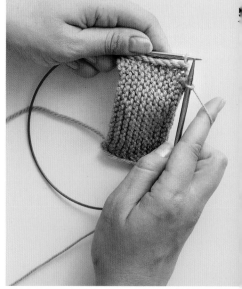

1. When you reach the end of your final row, turn the knitting around;

2. knit the first two stitches as usual. Instead of continuing, though,

3. use the tip of your nondominant needle to pick up the first stitch and pass it over the other;

4. you'll be left with just one stitch on the working needle. Continue in this way, knitting one stitch as usual and passing the farther one over it so you always have one stitch on your working needle,

5. until you've reached the very last stitch. Cut the yarn, leaving a tail of about 6 inches (15 cm), and pull it all through that last loop.

That's it! You've officially made your first piece of knitting. If you want to keep it, use the yarn (aka tapestry) needle (remember that?) to **weave in** the yarn ends. You can do this by threading the needle with the tail of yarn, and sewing it into the edge of the knitting, underneath the stitches. When you've tucked it under four or five times, trim the yarn so that it doesn't show. Do the same with the other tail.

Rip It Up

If you're not the sentimental type or would rather have the yarn for other purposes, forgo the final step of casting off; instead, leave that last stitch intact and do not cut the yarn. Remove the stitch from the needle and tug the yarn so that the stitch unknits itself; continue tugging until the knitting is entirely unraveled. You can wind the yarn back up into its original form. It might look a little worse for wear right now, but once it's had time to rest and has been properly knit up again, that will likely be unnoticeable.

This technique, this unknitting, is known in some circles as `frogging`, which is a play on the sound of the phrase "rip it, rip it, rip it." You can deploy it at any time in a knitting project, not just at the end, and it's useful if you've messed up beyond repair or if you hate your knitting so much that you would rather set it on fire than look at it for another minute. While I'd caution you to continue pushing through, at least so you can compare what you've been doing to what feels or looks better as you get the hang of it, I also understand that sometimes what your brain and hands need is a clean slate. In these cases, simply slide the stitches off the needle and gently pull the working yarn, winding it as you go.

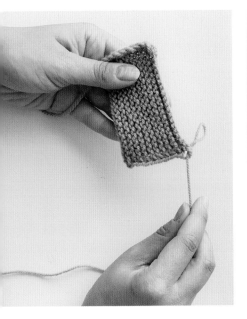 

You can frog an entire project or just unravel a couple of rows if you can see a spot where you'd like to pick it up again. The latter is a little trickier, since you'll need to carefully poke the needle back through the loops left by the stitches, which can result in dropping a few. But you can always knit your way back to those and pick them up, and most of the yarns I recommend above for the hat are sturdy enough that the stitches should hold their shape for a bit even without a needle.

Just know that if and when you do frog, you are part of a long line of knitters who have done so and will continue to do so no matter how experienced they may be. Unknitting is as much a part of the process as knitting.

- - - - - - - - - - - - - -

MAKING
THE HAT

- - - - - - - - - - - - - -

Odds are you have worn a hat before, and likely even contemplated its components: There's the stretchy **brim**, the cylindrical **body**, and the domed **top**. (It feels silly to put such simple words in boldface, but I value consistency over dignity.)

Each of these three sections will be knitted slightly differently from the others, and the difficulty will increase incrementally as you move through them. By the end, you should have not only a hat but a better working understanding of how knitting works, and how yarn can be manipulated to achieve various effects.

Again, I want to reiterate that if this is your very first project, it is probably not going to go smoothly. I say this not to scare you but to liberate you; as much as both of us want you to walk away with the ideal garment, the world's most thoughtful gift, the pinnacle of all human creativity, the pressure to make that happen can be enough to paralyze you or frustrate you into submission at the first tangled roadblock. If you can make one promise to yourself here, I suggest that it be to finish the project. Even if it's full of holes or looks better suited for a family of baby mice to live in, just get to the final stage, so you can see how it all fits together. Then you have my permission to unravel it, or to seek out that family of baby mice.

Materials to Make Your Hat

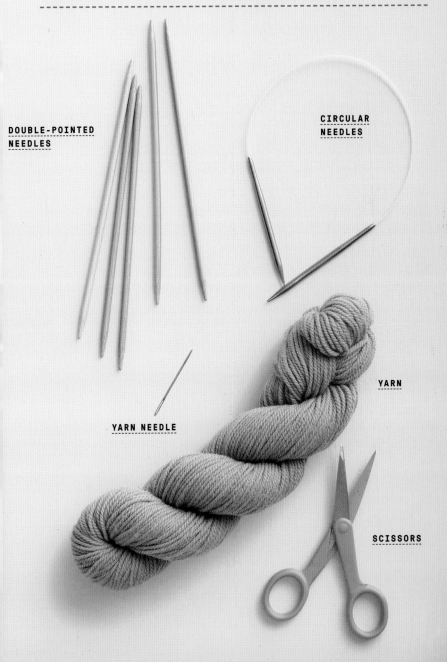

DOUBLE-POINTED
NEEDLES

CIRCULAR
NEEDLES

YARN

YARN NEEDLE

SCISSORS

The Pattern

This is really more of a hat recipe than a hard-and-fast
pattern, with plenty of room to make it your own. Still, on
the following pages is how the pattern looks written out,
so you can get used to deciphering pattern-speak and have
all the instructions in one place. I'll explain each step in
(possibly excruciating) detail, so just bookmark the pages
and don't worry if it seems like gobbledygook.

Cast on 80 (100, 120) stitches on a circular needle. Do not join in the round.

Knit 16 (20, 24) rows in garter stitch.

Join for working in the round. Knit 32 (40, 48) rounds in stockinette stitch.

*Knit 8 stitches, k2tog. Repeat from * all the way around.

Knit the following round.

*Knit 7 stitches, k2tog. Repeat from * all the way around.

Knit the following round.

*Knit 6 stitches, k2tog. Repeat from * all the way around.

Knit the following round.

*Knit 5 stitches, k2tog. Repeat from * all the way around.

(Slip all stitches to 3 double-pointed needles.)

Knit the following round.

*Knit 4 stitches, k2tog. Repeat from * all the way around.

Knit the following round.

*Knit 3 stitches, k2tog. Repeat from * all the way around.

Knit the following round.

*Knit 2 stitches, k2tog. Repeat from * all the way around.

Knit the following round.

*Knit 1 stitch, k2tog. Repeat from * all the way around.

Knit the following round.

K2tog all the way around.

Cut working yarn and pull through remaining stitches.
Seam up brim stitches. Weave in all loose ends and trim.

The Pattern

Knitting the Brim

The brim will determine how large the rest of the hat will be, which means you need to decide who it's for and figure out roughly what size their head is in order to know how many stitches to cast on. I am a lady with a relatively small head, so when I make one of these hats for myself I cast on 100 stitches for a snug fit, and 110 for a more drapey version. For my father, a man with a pretty big noggin, I cast on 120. For a friend's baby, I cast on 80.

I'd say those are fairly safe rules of thumb (small = 80, medium = 100, large = 120), but your tension could vary from mine, and your loved ones could have gorgeously out-of-the ordinary pates. Luckily, hats are stretchy, and unless we're wildly off base here your hat should still fit its intended recipient, or at least somebody in your life with a head. If you do choose an in-between number, I highly recommend sticking with multiples of 10 stitches for this first project. It'll make counting and keeping track of whether you've accidentally added or subtracted stitches much easier, and will help you out when we start to reduce stitches on purpose (known as **decreasing**) in the final stage.

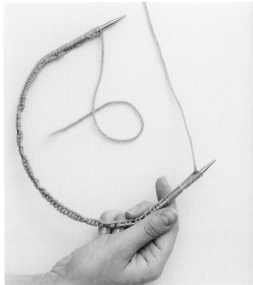

The brim of this particular hat is very similar to the practice swatch you just knitted, only longer and with potentially fewer rows. You'll be using your circular needle and knitting back and forth in rows, the way you did before, rather than connecting one end of the project to the other and knitting it **in the round**—that will come in the next phase, once you're comfortable with **knitting flat**.

So! Using the backwards loop method we went over earlier, cast on 80, 100, or 120 stitches. The cast-on should take up roughly the total real estate of your circular needle, from end to end (don't worry if it doesn't stretch all the way), and take care that the stitches don't slide off. You can count the stitches as you cast them on, or cast on a bunch of stitches and then count them. Then you can add more or take some away to get the exact number you want.

Turn the work around and knit all the way back. Repeat this about 16 times if you're making a small hat, which should result in 8 garter stitch ridges; 20 times if you're making a medium (so that's 10 ridges); and 24 times if you're shooting for large (12 ridges). This isn't a hard-and-fast rule by any means, so feel free to make your brim narrower or wider, as you see fit. I like how the hat looks proportionally with the suggested repeated rows, but the number of repeats won't affect fit in any real way, so go with what your heart tells you—and use this as a chance to get really comfortable with the knit stitch, since what's to come is a bit more complicated.

Knitting the Brim

Knitting the Body

At this point, you'll have a long strip of knitted fabric, which you've knitted flat. From here, we're going to progress to knitting in the round. This will require very little extra effort on your part. When you reach the end of the last brim row, instead of turning the work around and doubling back, continue knitting the stitches on what is currently your nondominant needle. It'll probably look a little sloppy at the spot where you join, but we can clean that up at the end.

I recommend adding a **stitch marker** at that spot, to demarcate where your **rounds** (which are the same as rows, but in circular knitting) begin. This isn't mandatory, but it will be helpful later on when you're doing your decreases and will want to know where you are within the project. You can just cut a small piece of yarn or string and tie it into a little knot, then slide it onto the needle between the stitches. When you reach it each round, slip it from one needle to the other as if you were knitting it, except without feeding it any yarn and just allowing it to jump.

I've also used safety pins, rings, rubber bands, and any number of other tiny nonsensical objects I've found on my person when I've decided I could use a stitch marker. There are also lovely ones sold explicitly for this purpose—always a good gift idea for a knitter—but, especially at this early stage, don't worry about buying anything extra.

For now, armed with the trusty knit stitch, continue knitting the body of the hat. You'll just keep going around and around in circles, acknowledging that you've started a new row when you slip your stitch marker and/or pass the break in the brim. (We'll seam that up at the end, unless you prefer a more avant-garde split look, in which case I would never cramp your style.) How many rows you knit is, again, a matter of preference; fewer rows mean a snugger cap, while more mean it'll be slouchier.

I like to double the number of rows I knit for the brim as a preliminary rule, so if you went with 20 (remember, that's 10 ridges), try knitting 40 rows for the body. You won't have ridges here, which I find easier to count, but you can always count the rows of stitches by each V to make sure you're still on track, and the Hat Police will not come to arrest you if you're off by one or two.

Knitting the Body

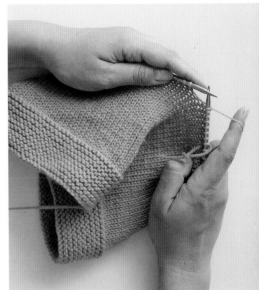

Sides and Stockinette Stitches

Even though you're continuing to knit the exact same stitch you've been doing all along, you'll doubtless notice that the way the fabric looks has changed. The reason for this is that the knit stitch doesn't look the same from both sides; one side is much smoother (the **right** side), while the other is bumpier (the **wrong** side, though it can look just as good if not better than the right side). Why, then, has your work up until now (the brim that you knitted flat) been so consistent (meaning if you turn it around, it looks the same from the back as it does from the front)?

The thing is, it's actually not the same front and back; those little ridges you've been producing are the "wrong" side of the knitting jutting out. Look closely at the brim and you'll see that, on either side, what looks from the front like a ridge looks from the back like a little divot. Not only is the fabric you've been knitting not, in fact, identical front and back; the right and wrong sides of the fabric are inverted from one another. The fabric is almost unnoticeably wavy, jutting one way and then the other, but so tightly joined together that it forms a sturdy whole.

This is also why, if you've attempted to pick up a dropped stitch, you might have noticed that the "trail" it left didn't look like the surrounding fabric. That's because you'd essentially left a series of knit stitches in what was actually an alternating pattern. (Again, don't trouble yourself too much with all this string theory. Full grasp of it is extremely *not* necessary to get this project done.)

When you knit in the round, though, you'll never have ridges on the right side, and each side will be uniform, since you're not turning the work around. The body rows on the right side of your hat will form a series of Vs (in contrast to the nubbly garter stitch fabric of the brim), while the back will look like a flatter version of the brim. This is known as **stockinette stitch**.

In order to achieve the same effect while knitting flat, you'd need to first knit a whole row, then purl your way back. As mentioned earlier, purling is the inverse of knitting; the back of a knit looks like a purl, and the back of a purl looks like a knit. As also mentioned earlier, I've found that purling can be too much to ask new knitters to wrap their heads around, since it's just similar enough to the knit stitch to throw you off before you're 100 percent confident about the first motion, and so, by design, this pattern doesn't involve purling. No offense to purling, but you can be kind of a drag.

The quasi-important thing about knitting the body is to make sure you've still got the same number of stitches you started with—I find that counting stitches in groups of 5 on the needle helps me keep track without spending interminable hours tallying. Keeping the right number of stitches going will put you in good shape for the final step: decreasing for the top of the hat.

Switching to a
New Ball of Yarn

If at any point you run out of yarn from one ball and have to switch over to the other, it's an easy process—just take the starting end of the yarn from the next ball and tie it loosely around the end of the old yarn, leaving a 6-inch (15-cm) tail from both, and weave those tails in at the end of the project. I prefer to do this at the very beginning of a new round even if that means ending the old ball a bit early, but it's not a big problem if you do it in the middle.

Knitting the Top

I hope the knitting here hasn't been too impossible. Even if you mess up from time to time, by this point you'll have knitted literally thousands of stitches and the motions are likely working their way into your hands.

I say all this to reassure you, as we enter the final and arguably most difficult stage of the hat, that you are fully capable of pulling it off. Even if you knew just these skills—casting on, the knit stitch, and casting off—you'd be able to make tons of projects. And what we're going to learn here, **decreasing** and **knitting on double-pointed needles**, is just an extension of what you've already been doing.

DECREASING

We'll begin with decreasing, which is exactly what it sounds like: steadily and evenly reducing the number of stitches per row so that the hat forms a dome shape, as opposed to the cylinder you've been knitting up till now. This will be accomplished by **knitting two stitches together**; it's abbreviated in knitting patterns as **k2tog**, which is a tattoo I perennially think about getting.

In order to make the slope of the hat nice and even, we'll be decreasing in a specific pattern. This is where the multiples of 10 stitches come in handy, because you'll have an easily divisible number to work with. (I'm sorry for the math! Knitting is not-so-secretly heavy on the math, but the numbers are intuitive enough, once you're in it, for even the most numerically challenged among us [hi].)

At this point, some kind of row demarcation becomes more important. If you have a strong sense of where the rounds begin, thanks to the break in the brim, cool, but if you find yourself zoning out or unsure, now is the time to add that stitch marker at the beginning of your next round.

Start by knitting 8 stitches as usual. Then, instead of knitting just the next stitch, put the tip of your working needle through the next 2 stitches (yes, 2), treating them as if they were 1; you can even pinch

Knitting the Top

95

them together with your free hand if that makes it easier to conceptualize. Knit your usual under-over-through motion (or picking, if you prefer Continental), and now, where you once had a set of 10 stitches, you have only 9.

Continue this until the end of the row: knitting 8 stitches as usual, then knitting 2 together. You'll know to stop doing this when you reach your marker. If you want to stop and count here, go for it. Just take your original number of cast-on stitches, divide it by 10, and subtract that from the original in order to determine how many you should have. So if you started with 100, you should now, at the end of your first decreased row, have 90. If you started with 110, you should have 99. Sorry if this seems like the most obvious math in the world to you! Or if, conversely, it seems unfathomably hard!

What should you do if you don't have the right number? Honestly, probably don't worry about it—if you're wildly off, say, you're missing 20 or 30 stitches from the original count, that might be some slight cause for concern and you should make sure that you're decreasing only two stitches at a time, and not doing it more frequently than you're supposed to. Otherwise, if you're off by, say, 4 or 5, it won't be obvious, especially considering this is the top of the hat. Just try to stay as on track as possible.

Knitting the Top

After you've worked this **decrease round**, knit the following round totally as usual. This makes the slope more gradual and also causes less stress on the fabric; knitting stitches together necessarily tugs on it and can leave small gaps, which knitting plain rows in between decrease rounds helps mitigate.

When you arrive back at the marker, this time you'll knit 7 stitches as usual and then knit 2 together, continuing all the way around.

Then knit all the way across the following round, as before.

After that comes a round of knit 6, knit 2 together, all the way around.

Then a round of knitting all the way across.

Then knit 5, knit 2 together, all the way around.

A few things should be happening by this point. First, you might be noticing a pattern emerging in the fabric—a series of raised stitches slowly forming even(ish) diagonal lines. Those are the decreases, and you can use the lines to "read" your knitting and see where the next decrease is coming even if you're not counting. It also looks pretty cool.

Second, you should also be noticing a feeling of tightness in your knitting, because as you lower your stitch count it'll be harder and harder to work with the length of your circular needle. Depending on what size hat you're knitting and your tension, this tightness can happen earlier or later in the decrease section, but no matter when it comes up you'll need to switch to your DPNs to complete the project.

Knitting the Top

Knitting the Top

MOVING TO THE DPNS

Knitting with DPNs looks a lot scarier and more complicated than it actually is. It's definitely a minor pain to work with four (or more!) needles, but you don't actually need to worry about holding all of them at once because they'll be firmly ensconced in the knitting. You'll still be focusing on just two—the one you're working with and the one holding the immediately upcoming stitches. The others can dangle there quietly until you need them.

To prepare, lay out your four DPNs in front of you (they usually come in sets of five and occasionally six, but you won't need all of those for this project, and it's nice to have a spare handy for when you inevitably lose or break one). You should perform this step before an all-knitting round, not a decrease round, so you have one less factor to keep track of when you pick it back up.

Your project will be divided across three needles, with the fourth acting as the working needle. You can divide the stitches a couple of ways, depending on how your brain works. You can just divide by 3, and put an equal number of stitches on each needle (plus or minus 1 if your stitch count is not a number that divides evenly). If you're at all nervous about working with DPNs and think that more math would break you, do this, and probably skip the opposite page for good measure.

In my knitting, I prefer to divide according to each set of decreases rather than the total number of stitches, so that each needle is a little self-contained unit of decreases. So say I started with 100 stitches and am now down to 60. That means I have 10 sets of 6 stitches and I'd like to keep those sets together. I'd likely put 3 sets of 6 stitches on the first needle (so 18 total), 4 sets on the second (24), and the final 3 sets on the last (18 again).

In order to get said stitches onto said needles, carefully slip them onto the nonworking needle and onto the first DPN, one by one. When you have your desired number of stitches on that needle, pick up the next DPN and do the same, letting the first one hang. Be careful not to let any stitches fall off, but you don't have to clutch the needle or anything like that; especially if you're using wood or bamboo DPNs, the stitches should stay where they are. Continue to the third needle, using a stitch marker to keep track of where your round starts.

Once you have fully transitioned to the DPNs, you can say good-bye to your circular needle. It might look kind of crazy to you, with all these pieces of wood sticking out of your project, but the procedure here is exactly the same as it was before, just with gaps between needles instead of one continuous row.

Using the fourth DPN as the working needle, knit a round as usual. When you reach the end of the stitches on a given DPN, just jump across to the next one and knit the stitches there. The working needle becomes a nonworking needle, and the nonworking needle becomes your new working needle. Once you've knitted the stitches on all three DPNs and arrived back at your stitch marker, you've completed the round. The needles will feel like they're getting in your way when they're not in use, and you'll have to worry about stitches sliding off the ends, but that's unfortunately just part of the challenge; the best strategy is to work on your tension, so that the stitches are snug enough on the needles that they won't flop around, and not so tight you can't work them. If you find that you're really having trouble with stitches making their escape, you can buy point protectors to put on the ends of the nonworking needles to keep them all in place.

 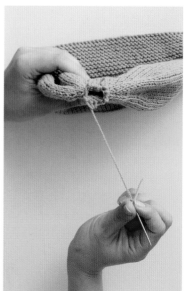

Continue the decrease pattern you'd been working on the circular needle. Knit 4 stitches, then knit 2 together, repeating all the way around.

Knit all the stitches in the following round.

Knit 3 stitches, then knit 2 together, repeating all the way around.

Knit all the stitches in the following round.

Knit 2 stitches, then knit 2 together, repeating all the way around.

Knit all the stitches in the following round.

Knit 1 stitch, then knit 2 together, repeating all the way around.

Knit all the stitches in the following round.

Knit 2 together all the way around.

By this point, you'll have very few stitches left on each needle (about a dozen or fewer), depending on how many you started with. Now we're going to **bind off**. To do this, cut the working yarn, leaving a tail of about 6 inches (15 cm) attached to the knitting. Use it to thread your yarn needle, and work that yarn needle through each of the loops still on the needles, removing the DPNs as you go. Pull the yarn tightly so that it creates a sort of drawstring, closing up the hole at the top of the hat. Turn the hat inside out and weave the yarn needle through some stitches a few times so that the yarn is secure, tying a knot or two if you're worried about it coming apart. Trim the loose end.

Finally, you're going to **seam up** the brim. Use the length of yarn dangling from the cast-on edge to thread your yarn needle. Keeping the hat inside out (this is so the seam is less visible), hold the two brim edges side by side. Work the yarn needle through the outermost garter ridges on each edge, connecting them together. It doesn't matter if it doesn't look perfect, so long as the edges are getting sewn up. When you reach the top of the brim, weave in the remaining yarn a few times. Trim the loose end. Turn the hat right side out

An optional final step for this project (and a nonnegotiable one for items like sweaters and socks) is to **block** your hat. This will help give it its final shape and work out some of the kinks in the fabric that might have occurred over the course of knitting it. It can also stretch the project somewhat if it's looking too small. Just lightly mist your project with water from a spray bottle or something similar, and gently pin the project to a towel in the shape you'd like it to be (in this case, that can mean literally balling the towel up in the shape of a head) or lay it out flat. Let it dry for about twenty-four hours.

(That said, I hardly ever block smaller accessories, so I'm telling you to block really just in order to do my due diligence as a knitting teacher.)

Modifications

There are myriad ways to spice up this most basic of hat patterns. We'll go over three: one that involves switching up the brim, one where you'll add stripes to the body, and one where you'll make a pom-pom for the top. Feel free to mix and match any of these components; I'd say they go from most to least difficult in the order described.

Ribbed Brim

Here, you'll use purl stitches to create a ribbed, stretchy brim. Instead of starting flat and working back and forth, you'll start in the round from the very beginning. And instead of using only knit stitches all the way around, you'll knit 2, then purl 2, and repeat.

Here's how the pattern looks:

Cast on 80 (100, 120) stitches on a circular needle. Join for working in the round.

*Knit 2 stitches, then purl 2 stitches. Repeat from * all the way around for 16 (20, 24) rounds.

Knit 32 (40, 48) rounds in stockinette stitch.

*Knit 8 stitches, k2tog. Repeat from * all the way around.

Knit the following round.

*Knit 7 stitches, k2tog. Repeat from * all the way around.

Knit the following round.

*Knit 6 stitches, k2tog. Repeat from * all the way around.

Knit the following round.

*Knit 5 stitches, k2tog. Repeat from * all the way around.

(Slip all stitches to 3 double-pointed needles.)

Knit the following round.

*Knit 4 stitches, k2tog. Repeat from * all the way around.

Knit the following round.

*Knit 3 stitches, k2tog. Repeat from * all the way around.

Knit the following round.

*Knit 2 stitches, k2tog. Repeat from * all the way around.

Knit the following round.

*Knit 1 stitch, k2tog. Repeat from * all the way around.

Knit the following round.

K2tog all the way around.

Cut working yarn and pull through remaining stitches.
Weave in all loose ends and trim.

Ribbed Brim

Stripes

The easiest way to make your knitting look more professional is to change up the colors. For this, you'll be knitting the hat exactly as written, only you'll need one skein each of two colors rather than two of the same; in the pattern, we'll call the color that makes up the bulk of the hat the **main color** (MC) and the color of the stripes the **contrasting color** (CC).

There are plenty of ways to add a color and to work with multiple colors while knitting, including many complicated knots and one method that requires spit. Here, we're going to keep it pretty quick and dirty, basically just jumping from one color to the other and tidying it up later.

When you reach the end of a round (thank goodness for stitch markers!), simply let the main color drop down the back of the work. With the contrasting color, tie a very loose knot around the main color, leaving a 6-inch (15-cm) tail and making sure you're still able to slide the knot up and down the working yarn of the main color. Start knitting with the new color, tightening up the knot periodically as you progress—it's okay if there's still something of an ugly gap, as you'll be seaming that up at the end.

The next time you need to change colors, from contrasting back to main, pick up the strand of the main color and loop it once around the working contrasting yarn, tight enough so that the fabric is smooth but not so much that it puckers. Continue knitting. When you reach the end of your project, use your yarn needle to weave in the tail where you first added the contrasting color; trim all loose ends.

The TL;DR of this is . . . knit until you want to switch colors, then knit with the new color, trying to minimize the gap between the colors. Frankly, however you can best visualize this, go for it.

You can choose how frequent and how wide you want your stripes to be. I find that it looks the most design-y to have thinner stripes less frequently, and that's what I've laid out here.

Stripes

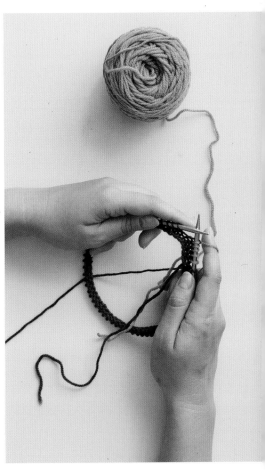

Cast on 80 (100, 120) stitches on a circular needle in the main color (MC). Do not join in the round.

Knit 16 (20, 24) rows in garter stitch.

Join for working in the round. Knit 5 rounds in MC, then switch to contrasting color (CC) for 3 rounds. Repeat this pattern 4 (5, 6) times, for a total of 32 (40, 48) rounds in stockinette stitch. Switch back to MC for the decrease rounds.

*Knit 8 stitches, k2tog. Repeat from * all the way around.

Knit the following round.

*Knit 7 stitches, k2tog. Repeat from * all the way around.

Knit the following round.

*Knit 6 stitches, k2tog. Repeat from * all the way around.

Knit the following round.

*Knit 5 stitches, k2tog. Repeat from * all the way around.

(Slip all stitches to 3 double-pointed needles.)

Knit the following round.

*Knit 4 stitches, k2tog. Repeat from * all the way around.

Knit the following round.

*Knit 3 stitches, k2tog. Repeat from * all the way around.

Knit the following round.

*Knit 2 stitches, k2tog. Repeat from * all the way around.

Knit the following round.

*Knit 1 stitch, k2tog. Repeat from * all the way around.

Knit the following round.

K2tog all the way around.

Cut working yarn and pull through remaining stitches.
   Seam up brim stitches. Weave in all loose ends and trim.

Stripes

Pom-pom

Pom-poms are ridiculously fun to make, and a wonderful way to use up extra yarn. Some methods involve forks or dedicated pom-pom-making implements; here, you're just going to use your fingers.

Pom-pom

With the desired yarn, wrap the center three fingers of your non-dominant hand—use a bunch of yarn, so much that it's hard to bend them; the more yarn, the fluffier the pom! Leave a tail of the yarn dangling so that it's still visible; 6 inches (15 cm) should be more than enough. Once you've reached your desired wrap-capacity, cut the yarn attached to the ball, and using the tail, carefully tie a very tight knot around the entire bundle vertically. Once it's been secured (you can tie a couple of knots to make sure), slide it all off your fingers, and use your scissors to cut through the loops on both sides, making extremely sure not to cut the knot holding it all together.

Pom-pom

You should have a sea anenome–looking thing at this point, so now comes the entertaining part: giving the pom-pom a haircut. Working over a trash can or paper bag, trim it on all sides so that it's even, fluffing as you go. You'll know it's done when it looks . . . like a pom-pom.

To attach it to your hat, thread your yarn needle with yarn left over either from the hat or from the pom-pom (you don't want it to be too obvious) and secure it with a few stitches through the very center of both the pom and the top of the hat. You'll want your stitches to be far enough apart that the pom-pom doesn't wobble; you can test it as you go. Tie off the yarn inside the hat and trim the loose ends.

Pom-pom

ENDNOTES

At this point, ideally, you've made a hat. Maybe you've made several! Maybe one turned out lumpy, and the next turned out stretched, and finally you arrived at a Goldilocks-ian equilibrium with a hat that fits, if not just right, then just right enough.

Maybe all of that happened completely out of order, and you're currently staring at the stocking cap or the yarmulke you birthed with no idea how it could be related to the perfect beanie you produced not two weeks before.

Maybe you just never quite cracked it at all.

What I hope is that you like the act of knitting. You don't have to love it, or feel like you're a natural at it; you don't even have to enjoy the hat pattern. My hope for you is that the motion, the under-over-through, the taking of very little and making something of substance, lingers in your fingers. I hope that you find yourself missing it when you're not doing it, even if the last time you touched your work in progress you threw it down in exasperation; I hope that you think, *Hey, this might be a nice time to knit* when you're stuck on the subway or watching a bland episode of television.

I hope that knitting adds something to your life, however small and fleeting. I hope that you'll arrive at your own views about which needles work best, and which types of yarn, and whether hats or scarves or, I don't know, potholders are better for beginners to attempt. I hope you teach somebody else, or at least encourage them to try.

That, above all, is what I hope: that you try. That you punch through the frustration, grit your teeth through the slog, and allow yourself to surrender to the repetitive motion of something that's been happening since long before us and will continue once we're gone. I hope you make hats for yourself and for everyone you love, and for the people you think you might someday grow to love. I hope you stay warm.

OTHER RESOURCES

This book is a small collection of my own twenty-plus years of experiences and best practices, as a student and a teacher and a messer-arounder, and certainly wouldn't exist without the guiding influence of countless knitters before me. Not to duck responsibility, or to burden you with buying a bunch of new books and patterns once you've finished with this one, but if you're thirsting for where to turn next, here are some ideas.

First, if you have even the slightest interest in the internet whatsoever, get a free account on **Ravelry** (ravelry.com). Ravelry is one part social network, one part pattern resource, one part yarn database, and probably a bunch of other parts I'm either forgetting about or don't look at regularly. You can use the site to connect with other knitters (and crocheters!), find patterns both free of charge and for a small cost that goes back to the designers, keep a record of the projects you've made and the yarn you've bought, and generally trawl around for inspiration. It's also an excellent place to ask questions—there's a huge array of forums, as well as a comments section for each individual pattern where designers and other knitters will often be on hand to help troubleshoot.

Second, here is a woefully incomplete list of pattern designers, writers, small business owners, and generally yarn-y people to keep an eye out for, as well as publications. I hope they will inspire you and enhance your sense of what it's possible to create with fiber and not just make you wildly jealous, the way they sometimes do me.

PATTERN DESIGNERS

Louis Boria
@brooklynboyknits

Hannah Fettig
knitbot.com

Anna Hrachovec
mochimochiland.com

Jessie Mae Martinson
@jessssiemae

Jeanette Sloan
@jeanettesloan

Meg Swansen &
Elizabeth Zimmermann
schoolhousepress.com

Stephen West
westknits.com

ONLINE RESOURCES

Mason-Dixon Knitting
masondixonknitting.com

Purl Soho
purlsoho.com

PUBLICATIONS

Amirisu

Interweave Knits

Knitscene

Knitty

Pompom Quarterly

Vogue Knitting

We Are Knitters by Alberto
Bravo and Pepita Marín

The Knit Vibe
by Vicki Howell

Knitlandia by Clara Parkes

You Can Knit That
by Amy Herzog

ACKNOWLEDGMENTS

Thanks (and infinite yarn) to my wonderful agent, Kate McKean, who has been a friend, a cheerleader, a crafting buddy, and an unstoppable force throughout my career.

Thanks to Meredith A. Clark for dreaming this book into existence and helping me get it where I wanted it to be, and to the entire team at Abrams for their tireless work when it comes to making beautiful, functional things. Thanks also to Alexandra Grablewski, whose gorgeous photos make me feel like the knitting rock star I've always longed to be.

Thanks to all my fiber friends, in New York and beyond, who have made me feel so accepted in what I once thought was a solitary pursuit, and who teach me every day.

Thanks to Julia Rubin, Meredith Haggerty, and the rest of my coworker-pals at Vox Media, for their flexibility, their support, and their near-constant source of light and love even in dark times.

Finally, thanks to Brendan, who patiently lets me leave yarn everywhere.